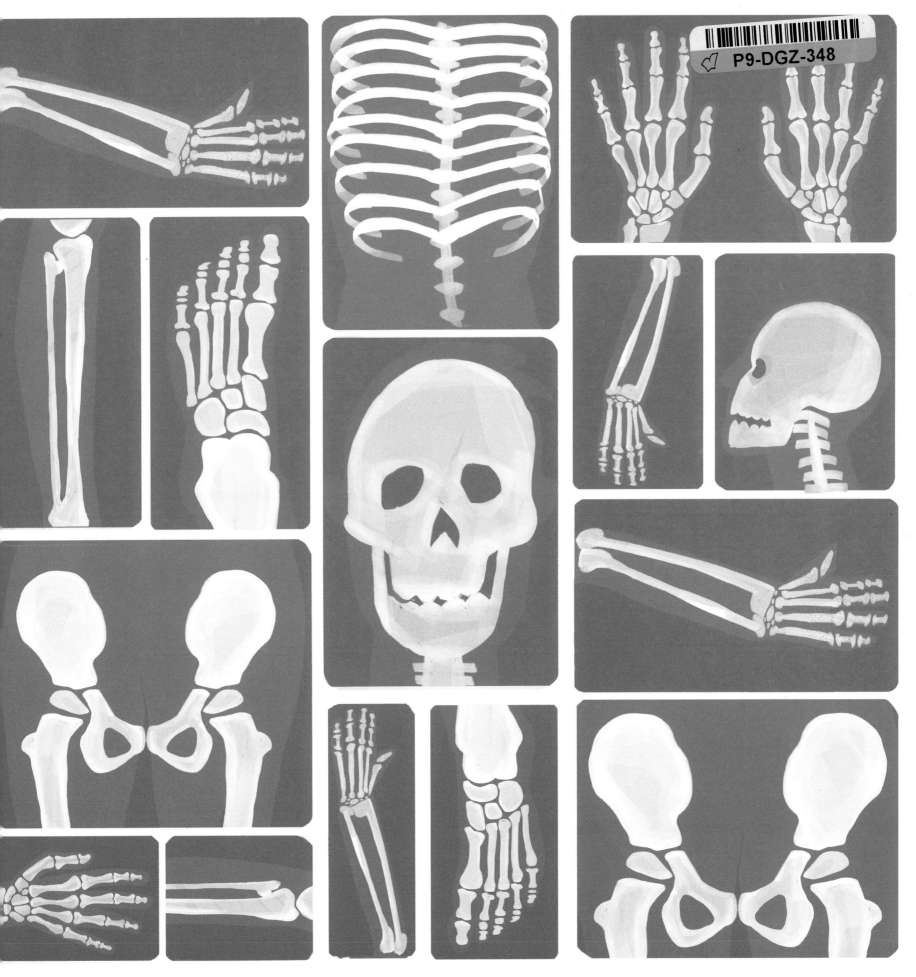

AT THE HOSPITAL

Carron Brown

Illustrated by Ipek Konak

Kane Miller
A DIVISION OF EDC PUBLISHING

A hospital is a busy place where you will find lots of different people doing all sorts of different jobs.

If you look closely in the rooms and hallways, you'll see doctors, paramedics, housekeepers and many others busy at work.

Shine a flashlight behind the page, or hold it up to the light to reveal the hidden sights of the hospital. Discover a world of great surprises.

It's the beginning of a busy day at the hospital. This woman has arrived at the reception desk. She is going to have a baby.

Who is behind the desk?

It's the receptionist.

Tap!
Tap!

The receptionist takes a patient's
details, and tells them where in
the hospital they need to go.

A nurse has brought the woman to
the Labor and Delivery unit.

Take a look inside.

In the room there is a special bed that can tilt up or down, a comfy chair and a television.

In a different part of the hospital,
this boy has made some new friends.

What room are they in?

They are in the playroom.

There are toys and games for
patients to play with. It's fun!

This girl has come to the hospital for an operation. She will be staying overnight.

What's in her bedside table?

A toothbrush and toothpaste,
a hairbrush, a book, some
photographs and a
pair of pajamas.

She has brought things that
will make her comfortable
during her stay.

An ambulance brings a sick or injured person to the hospital in an emergency.

This ambulance has been driven to the hospital by a paramedic.

Can you see what's inside?

There's a bed on wheels called a
stretcher, and lots of special equipment.

Another paramedic is checking that
there are medicines, dressings and
bandages ready for the next trip.

It's almost time for the girl's operation. She has had some medicine and feels sleepy.

What's behind the door?

It's the operating room. Inside, there's
a surgeon, an anesthesiologist and a nurse.

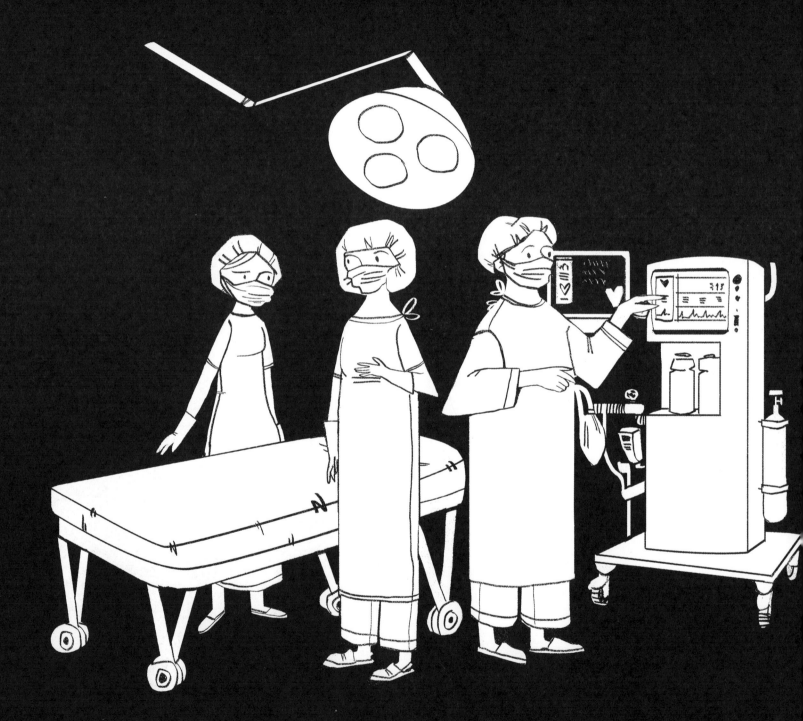

A nurse is helping the woman get comfortable.

She will be having her baby soon.

Where's the baby now?

The baby is inside her mom's tummy. She has been growing here for nine months, and is almost ready to be born.

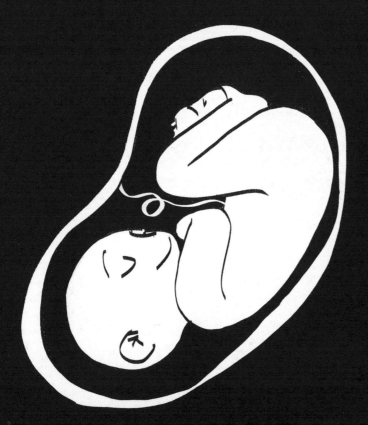

In another room in the hospital, this boy is having blood drawn for tests.

Where's the blood taken from?

The blood is taken from a vein.
Veins are like tubes in the body
that carry blood to the heart. The
heart pumps blood to all parts
of the body through different
tubes called arteries.

Doctors will look at the blood
to check the boy's health.

Sometimes, doctors are on call.
This means they are ready to help the
nurses with any patients that need them.

What's this room?

Yawn!

It's the on-call room.

Doctors can rest here until
they are needed.

This boy has a cast on his arm. He is choosing a color for the final layer.

Why does he need the cast?

An X-ray shows that a
bone in his arm is broken.

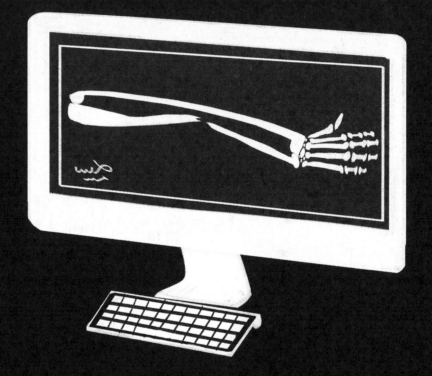

The hard cast will keep the bone in
the right position so it can heal.

Patients, visitors and hospital staff all stop by the cafeteria to grab a snack or to enjoy a meal.

Where's the food?

Here it is!

The hospital cooks work
with dieticians to make lots
of delicious and healthy
meals for everyone
to enjoy.

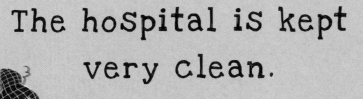

The hospital is kept very clean.

Where do these laundry bags go?

Whee!

The laundry bags drop down a chute, to a room at the bottom of the hospital.

The laundry will be washed and dried so it can be used again.

Look who's awake! After the operation, the girl has been asleep most of the day. Now, she's hungry.

What's for dinner?

There's a sandwich, some fruit
salad and a carton of milk.

Yum!

The woman's family has come to visit. Everyone is happy because ...

... the baby has been born!

She is only one-day old and
she is asleep in her bassinet.

It's nighttime, and the girl is asleep. The main lights are switched off, but a night-light gives off a gentle glow.

Who does the girl have with her?

Teddy is here.

The girl will sleep until
morning, when it will
be time to leave.

Good morning!

Everyone is happy to be going home.

Another busy day is about to begin
at the hospital.

There's more ...

Take a closer look around the hospital.

Paramedic A paramedic cares for a sick or injured person in an emergency, and takes them to the hospital in the ambulance for more treatment.

Stethoscope A doctor or nurse can listen to sounds in the body, such as a heartbeat, using a stethoscope. The round, flat part of the stethoscope is placed on the body, and the sound travels up through rubber tubes to earpieces worn by the doctor or nurse.

Surgeon A doctor who performs an operation is called a surgeon. An operation happens in a place called an operating room. During an operation, the surgeon is helped by nurses and the anesthesiologist.

Anesthesiologist Anesthesia is medicine that makes a patient sleep throughout surgery. The doctor who gives anesthetic to a patient is called an anesthesiologist. The anesthesiologist makes sure that the patient is comfortable during an operation.

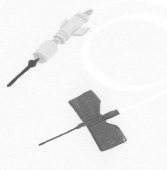

Butterfly needle A butterfly needle is a short needle with winglike handles, attached to a plastic tube. Blood from a vein is drawn up the tube into a container, so it can be tested in a laboratory, or by a hematologist, a doctor who studies blood.

X-ray An X-ray is a picture of the inside of the body. It is used to check if there are problems, such as broken bones or illnesses, that need to be treated. The person who takes an X-ray is called an X-ray technician.

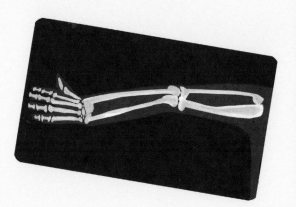

Cast A cast protects the area around a broken bone, and keeps the bone in the right place so it can heal. It is wet when first put on, but when it dries, it becomes very hard. A cast must be worn for several weeks, and is removed when the bone is healed.

First American Edition 2018
Kane Miller, A Division of EDC Publishing

Copyright © 2018 Quarto Publishing plc

For information contact:
Kane Miller, A Division of EDC Publishing
PO Box 470663
Tulsa, OK 74147-0663
www.kanemiller.com
www.edcpub.com
www.usbornebooksandmore.com

Library of Congress Control Number: 2017942239

Printed in China

ISBN: 978-1-61067-664-9

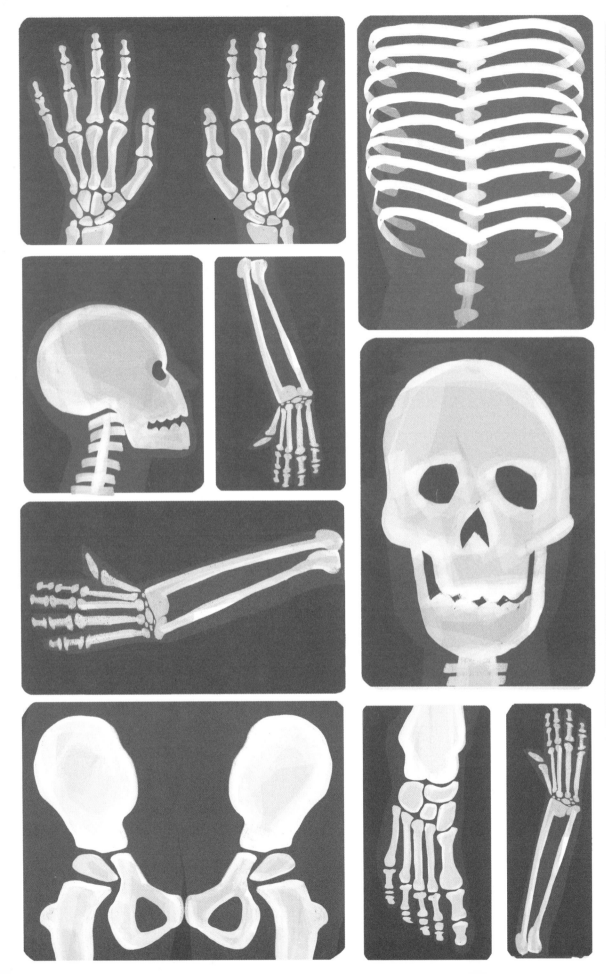
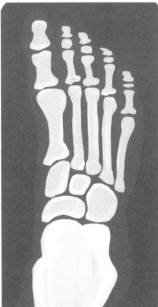
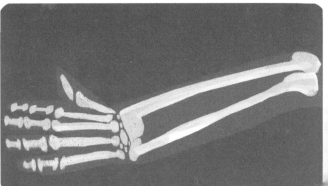
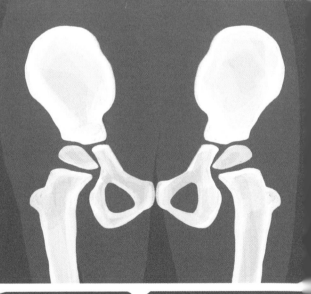
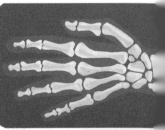